D1374050

Scott Ritter is a former UN Weapons Inspector (UNSCOM) in Iraq, and before that was in the US Marines. He is a Republican, he voted for George Bush, but is a vocal opponent of the impending war. He is much in the news.

William Rivers Pitt is an expert on the Middle East and an activist. He lives in Boston, USA.

*The photograph on the back cover is of
Iraqi civilians building mass graves.*

WAR
ON IRAQ

WAR

WHAT TEAM BUSH DOESN'T WANT YOU TO KNOW

ON IRAQ

SCOTT RITTER
FORMER UN WEAPONS INSPECTOR

and

WILLIAM RIVERS PITT

P

PROFILE BOOKS

First published in Great Britain in 2002 by
PROFILE BOOKS LTD
58A Hatton Garden
London ECIN 8LX
www.profilebooks.co.uk

First published in the United States of America by
Context Books, New York
www.contextbooks.com

3 5 7 9 10 8 6 4 2

Printed and bound in Great Britain by
Bookmarque Ltd., Croydon, Surrey

The moral right of the author has been asserted.

A CIP catalogue record for this book is available from the
British Library.

ISBN 1 86197 636 4

CONTENTS

"How is the world ruled and led to war?
Diplomats lie to journalists and believe these
lies when they see them in print."

Karl Kraus

WAR
ON IRAQ

A SPLENDID LITTLE ARMAGEDDON

"Today, every inhabitant of this planet must contemplate the day when this planet may no longer be habitable. Every man, woman and child lives under a nuclear sword of Damocles, hanging by the slenderest of threads, capable of being cut at any moment by accident or miscalculation or madness."

John F. Kennedy

The myth of the Gordian knot dates back to the days of Alexander the Great, whose conquests between 336 and 323 B.C. covered Asia Minor, Syria, Egypt, Babylonia, and Persia. As the story goes, King Gordius of Phrygia tied a knot that was so intricate it could not be unraveled. Alexander learned through an oracle that the next ruler of Asia would be the man who was able to undo this knot. Drawing his blade, Alexander sliced through the famous knot, solving the riddle with the edge of his sword.

Today, George W. Bush and his administration face another tangled knot. It is called Iraq, and no ancient king tied it. It was tied by America's involvement in the Middle East, which dates back decades, and by leaders in that area – among them the Shah of

Iran, the Ayatollah Khomeni, and of course Saddam Hussein. American presidents from Truman to Nixon, Carter, Reagan, Clinton, and two men named Bush tied this knot. It is an old jumble, tied as much by the Cold War as by oil, blood, and power.

The Gordian knot was broken with a sword. By using the sword to undo the knot of Iraq, the Bush administration will become ruler of nothing but chaos. The potential for a global conflagration lies in the actions Bush and his people are presently undertaking.

Bush and his administration have invested a lot of political capital in the war with Iraq, and the removal of Saddam Hussein. Backing down from this commitment will cost Bush enormously, making war inevitable. Richard Perle, chairman of the Defense Advisory Board and one of the architects of this war, bluntly stated that Bush must go to war in Iraq to preserve his political reputation. Commenting in the *New York Times* in August, Perle said, "The failure to take on Saddam after what the president said would produce such a collapse of confidence in the president that it would set back the war on terrorism."

According to Bush and the men who are pushing him towards this war – Defense Secretary Donald Rumsfeld, Deputy Defense Secretary Paul Wolfowitz, and Richard Perle – the process will be simplicity itself. Recall the ease with which we defeated Iraq in the first Gulf War. The United States will institute a "regime change" in Iraq, and bring forth the birth of a new democracy in the region. Along the way, we will remove Saddam Hussein, a man who absolutely, positively has weapons of mass destruction, a man who will use these weapons against his neighbors because he has done so in the past, a man who will give these terrible weapons to Osama bin Laden for use against America.

A fairly cut-and-dried case, no? America is more than prepared to listen to these pleasing arguments about evil in black and white, particularly after the horrors of September 11th. Few can contemplate in comfort the existence of chemical, biological, and nuclear weapons in the hands of a madman like Saddam Hussein. The merest whisper that he might give these weapons to Qaeda terrorists is enough to rob any rational American of sleep. Saddam has been so demonized in the American media – ever since the first President Bush compared him to Hitler – that they believe the case has been fully and completely made for his immediate removal.

Yet facts are stubborn things, as John Adams once claimed while successfully defending British redcoats on trial for the Boston Massacre. We may hate someone with passion, and we may fear them in our souls, but if the facts cannot establish a clear and concise basis for our fear and hatred, if the facts do not defend the actions we would take against them, then we must look elsewhere for the basis of that fear. Simultaneously, we must take stock of those stubborn facts, and understand the manner in which they define the reality – not the rhetoric – of our world.

The case for war against Iraq has not been made. This is a fact. It is doubtful in the extreme that Saddam Hussein has retained any functional aspect of the chemical, nuclear, and biological weapons programs so thoroughly dismantled by the United

Nations weapons inspectors who worked tirelessly in
Iraq for seven years. This is also a fact. The idea that
Hussein has connections to fundamentalist Islamic
terrorists is laughable – he is a secular leader who has
worked for years to crush fundamentalist Islam
within Iraq, and if he were to give weapons of any
kind to Qaeda, they would use those weapons on
him first.

The coalition that came together for the Gulf
War is nonexistent today, and a vast majority of the
international community stands furiously against another war on Iraq. If Bush decides unilaterally to attack, he will be in violation of international law. If
Bush does attack Iraq, he will precipitate the exact
conflict of cultures between the West and Islam that
Osama bin Laden was hoping for when his agents
flew three planes into the World Trade Center and
the Pentagon. An attack on Iraq could bring about a
wider world war America cannot afford, and that a
vast majority of Americans do not desire. These are
facts.

There is no question that Saddam Hussein is one
of the most wretched men to foul the skin of the
earth. He rules in the mode of any tyrant, by fear and
violence. Were he able, he would surely attack Iran,
Kuwait and Saudi Arabia – not to mention Israel – to
augment his power in the region. Herein lies the rub:
The economic sanctions have rendered his conventional weaponry impotent by denying him access to
the spare parts that are essential to any functioning
mechanized military. The UNSCOM inspectors destroyed, right to the ground, any and all capabilities
he possessed to create weapons of mass destruction.

He has no connections whatsoever to the terrorists who struck America on September 11th. Saddam Hussein is not capable of acting upon any of his desires, real or imagined. He does not have the horses.

We must come to a disturbing conclusion, based on the facts at hand. Saddam Hussein is a monster, by any definition, but he is our monster. He is as much an American creation as Coca-Cola and the Oldsmobile. Our government supported his regime during his war with Iran, a war in which he used chemical weapons on the battlefield with our full knowledge, with our arms, money, and military intelligence. The United States did not remove him during the Gulf War, and in fact thwarted attempts by Iraqi insurgents – inspired to act by our rhetoric – to overthrow his regime.

We must see the cultural dynamic of Iraq for what it is. All of the Bush administration's talk of "regime change" and democracy in Iraq ignores the realities on the ground there. Western-style democracy – majority rules – is antithetical to our national interests. The majority in Iraq, the Shiites, are ideologically and theologically tied to Iran. Allowing this group to rule in Iraq would forge a bond of fundamentalist ideology with Iran, located right on top of all that strategically necessary oil. We cannot allow the Kurds, who make up 23% of the population, to rule. The neighboring Turks, who have been fighting the Kurds, simply will not allow it. The remaining 17% of the population are the Sunnis, as is Hussein. The Sunni tribes control Iraq now, and a regime change would find its new leader from among this group. The brutal dynamics of Sunni tribalism in Iraq guarantee that a new leader from this section of Iraq would rule as brutally, or more brutally, than Hussein.

We helped to create the monster, and we are stuck with him. War on Iraq would enflame the Middle East to such a disastrous degree that the war on terror would spin out of control. Further terrorist attacks on America would be a foregone conclusion. We will not get approval from the United Nations or the international community for this war, and our unilateral action will disgrace us across the globe. Even if we were able to depose Saddam Hussein without that region flying apart at the seams, his replacement would be no better.

The only solution requires time, patience, and the loss of some political capital for George W. Bush. Cultural change in Iraq will take decades, and will not happen at all while the people live in poverty. We must lift the sanctions against Iraq, and allow its people to become once again the first world nation they were before Hussein's disastrous engagements with Iran and Kuwait. In exchange for this largesse, which would be a mercy to the civilians, Saddam Hussein must accept without precondition the reinsertion of U.N. weapons inspectors. This will guarantee that Hussein cannot develop any technology that threatens the region or America. As the standard of living improves for Iraqi civilians, as a viable middle class is created, the cultural and economic schisms that have defined Iraq will begin to disappear. The power of Saddam Hussein will wane.

The alternative is a disastrous war, tens of thousands of civilian casualties, hundreds or thousands of American casualties, the condemnation of the international community, a deadly explosion of rage in the Muslim world, and a new Iraqi leader who will in no way be an improvement over the current one.

This book was written to provide a compendium of the "stubborn facts" that surround this dubious war with Iraq, and the long history we share with that nation. The backbone of this book is an interview with W. Scott Ritter, one of the most knowledgeable men on the planet regarding the history, politics, and potential armament of Iraq. For seven years, Mr. Ritter was a weapons inspector in Iraq, tasked to destroy Hussein's weapons of mass destruction program.

From 1988 to 1990, Ritter performed arms control inspections in the former Soviet Union, developing a reputation for being both an excellent intelligence officer and an effective arms inspector. In August of 1990, after Iraq invaded Kuwait, Ritter was assigned by the Commandant of the Marine Corps to a special planning cell focused on Marine Corps combat options in Iraq. In December of that year, he was detached to Saudi Arabia, where he was assigned to General Norman Schwartzkopf's staff as an intelligence officer responsible for tracking SCUD missiles. He finished the Gulf War working with various Special Forces units devising concepts to interdict missile launches from Iraq into Israel. He left the Marine Corps in June of 1991, fully intending to find work in the private sector.

Fate, however, intervened. Mr. Ritter was contacted in 1991 by one of his former supervisors from his time performing weapons inspections in the Soviet Union, Army colonel Doug Englund. Citing his expertise in arms control and weapons inspections,

Englund invited Ritter to join UNSCOM – the United Nations Special Commission – authorized by Security Council Resolution 687 in April of 1991 to ensure that any and all weapons of mass destruction capability was destroyed in Iraq. In the end, Scott Ritter spent seven years pursuing and removing weapons of mass destruction in Iraq, as well as all production facilities, equipment, and delivery systems.

Mr. Ritter's time with UNSCOM came to a controversial conclusion in 1998, the details of which are described in my interview with him. He has argued vehemently before assembled groups, on television, and on radio, against the Bush administration's stance towards Iraq. For doing so, he has been labeled a traitor and an Iraqi agent.

Mr. Ritter is a patriot, a man with an astounding record of service to his country. He is a card-carrying Republican who voted for Bush in the 2000 election. Far more than any of the men who now push for the war on Iraq in Washington D.C., Mr. Ritter is a man who has seen the situation firsthand. He knows the weapons capabilities of Saddam Hussein, and believes there is no basis for war on the grounds cited by the Bush administration. Scott Ritter has seen the elephant. He knows the territory well. The "stubborn facts" that comprise his experience should be required reading for us all before we are set on a course that will almost certainly end in disaster.

Decide for yourself.

IRAQ IN THE 20TH CENTURY: A BRIEF HISTORY

> "I saw the Arab map.
> It resembled a mare shuffling on,
> dragging its history like saddlebags,
> nearing its tomb and the pitch of hell."
>
> *Ali Ahmed Said, Syrian poet*

Iraq is an industrialized nation of more than 20 million people. It is bordered to the north by Turkey and Syria, to the west is Jordan, Saudi Arabia and Kuwait form its southern border, and to the east is Iran. Iraq is almost completely landlocked; the area around Umm Qasr offering Iraq's only access to the Persian Gulf. Two hundred miles to the west of Iraq's border sits Israel, Lebanon, and the Mediterranean Sea.

The effects of Western colonialism, U.S. intervention, dangerous leadership, the Cold War, and oil dominated the history of Iraq during the twentieth century. Iraq holds the second largest proven stores of petroleum in the world, making it a sweet plum for Western industrialized nations.

In 1917, British forces invaded Mesopotamia and occupied Iraq, making it a British Mandate. Rebellions against the British in Iraq were put down by systematic aerial bombardment, the first time in history such tactics were used. It would not be the last. The borders that define Iraq today, along with the borders of most other Middle Eastern nations, were drawn arbitrarily by the British and the French in the early part of the century. These men who carved up the territory knew nothing of and cared little for the tribal connections that are the cultural essence of the Middle East.

In 1921, the British Colonial Office drew a new line in the sand, carving a border across southern Iraq to create the nation of Kuwait. This was done to deprive Iraq of access to the Persian Gulf. Seventy years later, when Saddam Hussein invaded Kuwait, he claimed the little nation state was always part of Iraq. When considering the British penchant for drawing and redrawing maps in the region, there appears to have been merit to his claim, if not to the actions it precipitated.

In 1932, Iraq was a recognized sovereign state and joined the League of Nations. The king remained a British creation, however. It was here the chaos that has dominated modern Iraq truly began.

In the years immediately after the end of World War II, a newly powerful America began to consider with cold pragmatism where its own self-interest lay. American policy in the Middle East, a policy that has existed to this day, a policy that has played an enormous part in the recent history of the region, can be summed up succinctly in the words of famed U.S. State Department official George Kennan, when in 1948 he said, "The U.S. has about 50% of the world's wealth but only 6.3% of its population. In this situation we cannot fail to be the object of envy and resentment. Our real task in the coming period is to devise a pattern of relationships which will permit us to maintain this position of disparity without positive detriment to our national security. To do so we will have to dispense with all sentimentality and day-dreaming, and our attention will have to be concentrated everywhere on our immediate national objectives. We need not deceive ourselves that we can afford the luxury of altruism and world benefaction. We should cease to talk about such vague and unreal objectives as human rights, the raising of living standards and democratization. The day is not far off when we are going to have to deal in straight power concepts. The less we are then hampered by idealistic slogans, the better."

This hard-eyed assessment of U.S. priorities came fully into play in 1951, when Dr. Mohammed Mossadegh took power in neighboring Iran and declared that Iran would retain full control of its own oil resources. Within the next two years, Mossadegh was deposed and the Shah of Iran installed, due in large part to support provided to the coup leaders by the CIA. Upon his installation, the Shah received assistance from American General Norman Schwartzkopf, Sr., father of the famed American General of the Gulf War, in the formation of the fearsome SAVAK Secret Police. The Shah became a puppet of U.S. interests, and the people of Iran began a long bout of suffering under his rule.

Across the border in Iraq, a man named Saddam Hussein was at the beginning of what became a long, bloody journey through the politics of power. Born in

1937, Hussein joined the socialist Ba'athist party in 1956. In 1958, the British-installed King of Iraq was overthrown in a popular revolt by Abd al-Quassim. In 1959, Hussein was one of the assassins involved in an attempted coup against Quassim, who was wounded in an attack. The coup failed, Hussein took a bullet in the leg, and was forced to flee the country to Syria, and then to Egypt.

The years between 1963 and 1968 were chaotic for Iraq. Another CIA-aided coup overthrew Quassim, and the Ba'athist party briefly took control of the nation. In 1968, Saddam Hussein helped lead another revolt, which made General Ahmed Hassan Bakr leader of Iraq. The Ba'ath Party was in control for good, and Hussein was named vice president. From this position of power, Hussein developed a vast network of secret police, designed to root out and destroy dissidents.

General Bakr nationalized Iraqi oil in 1972. President Richard Nixon immediately began to plot the reversal of this declaration, as America had done when Iran nationalized its oil in 1951. Nixon, along with the Shah, orchestrated the arming of Iraqi Kurds against Bakr. Iraq was placed on America's list of nations that sponsor terrorism.

This course of action was abruptly halted in 1975 when then Vice President Hussein and the Shah reached an agreement that ceded control of the strategically vital Shatt-al-Arab waterway in the Persian Gulf to Iran. In retrospect, it seems all too clear that Iraq's control of this waterway was the primary concern behind America's agitation against Iraq. Once the American-controlled Shah owned this passage to the Gulf, all American support to the Kurds ceased entirely. In commenting on this, Henry Kissinger stated, "Covert operations should not be confused with missionary work." Under Nixon, the arming of Iran by the United States was dramatically stepped up.

The conflict that erupted between Iran and Iraq cannot be fully understood unless the imperatives of the Cold War are completely appreciated. The United States dreaded the rise of Soviet influence in the region, given the strategic importance of the vast petroleum reserves there. With the Shah fully under the control of the United States, and with Iran in control of the Shatt-al-Arab waterway, U.S. interests in the region were safe. Declassified documents from the National Security Archive (see Appendix I) make it all too clear that concern regarding Soviet influence dominated U.S. behavior in the region.

1979 became a year that changed everything in the region, and conflict between America and Iraq became assured. The Shah of Iran was deposed, overthrown by a popular revolt fueled by nationalism, anti-American sentiment, and fundamentalist Islamic rhetoric. The Ayatollah Khomeni took power, setting the stage for decades of tension and strife with America. During the coup, the American embassy in Iran was overrun by insurgents, and the American diplomats within were taken hostage. For 440 days they were held, bound and blindfolded, to be paraded before cameras broadcasting the humiliation of America around the world. This hostage crisis assured continued enmity between Iran and America, and was the central factor in the electoral defeat of President Carter by Ronald Reagan in 1980.

Almost simultaneously, Saddam Hussein overthrew General Bakr and took full control of Iraq. His all-encompassing influence over the Ba'ath Party became cemented in one bloody day. Hussein convened all of the major powerbrokers in the party into one room. These men sat in terrified silence as Hussein read aloud the names of all his rivals in the Party. Those named were hustled from the room by secret police loyal to Hussein, brought outside, and shot. From that day forth, a challenge to Hussein's rule was rarely undertaken.

In the aftermath of this upheaval, American National Security Advisor Zbignew Brzezinski publicly encouraged Iraq to attack Iran and take back the Shatt-al-Arab waterway. With the Ayatollah in control of Iran, Soviet influence in that nation increased dramatically. The "Carter Doctrine" was established in 1980, stating that America would intervene militarily in the region to assure its access to the oil. In that same year, Saddam Hussein's armies invaded Iran, instigating a ruinous war that lasted for eight long years. The invasion was prompted as much by American urging as it was by Hussein's dislike for Islamic fundamentalism and his desire to control Iranian oil.

There was a sea change in relations between America and Iraq when Ronald Reagan became president. Fearing the rise of Soviet influence in Iran, and fearing an Iranian takeover of the region, the Reagan administration began actively arming and supporting Saddam Hussein. By 1982, Iraq was removed from the list of terrorist sponsoring nations. By 1984, America had restored full diplomatic relations with Iraq, and was actively sharing military intelligence with Hussein's army. This aid included arming Iraq with potent weapons, providing satellite imagery of Iranian troop deployments and tactical planning for battles, assisting with air strikes, and assessing damage after bombing campaigns.

It was during the Reagan years that the seeds of our current crisis were sown. American involvement became murky, morally ambiguous and two-faced to the extreme. In several aspects, it became patently illegal. American fears of a powerful Iran motivated policies that ignored terrible actions perpetrated by Iraq. At the same time, American interests in the rest of the world motivated the Reagan administration to provide illegal military support to Iran, even as it aided Iraq in the war.

The *New York Times* published a report in August of 2002 detailing statements by senior military officers involved with aiding Iraq during the Reagan administration. These officers claim that the Reagan administration was fully aware that Saddam Hussein was using chemical weapons against Iran, but continued to support him regardless. President Reagan, Vice President Bush, and several senior national security aides supported the covert program that provided American military assistance to Iraq, even as they knew that Iraq was using chemical weapons on the battlefield.

In early 1988, the Iraqi army, with American intelligence assistance, retook the Fao Peninsula, once again giving them access to the Persian Gulf. Defense intelligence officers visited the battlefield, where they found areas marked off as having been chemically contaminated. Containers of the drug atropine were scattered all about, having been clearly used by Iraqi soldiers to inoculate them against chemical weapons in the event they should blow back across their lines. 1988 was the same year that Saddam Hussein reportedly used chemical weapons against the Kurds in Halabja, an action roundly condemned at the time by U.S. officials. These same officials knew Hussein had been using chemical weapons against Iran, but had continued to support him. The battlefield use of these chemical weapons, and their purported use against the Kurds, is a fundamental part of the basis for George W. Bush's claims that Saddam Hussein must be attacked and removed.

In the middle of the conflict, the Reagan administration began covertly dealing with Iran in order to secure the release of a number of hostages being held by the Ayatollah's government. Arms, including 1,000 TOW missiles, were sold to Iran, and the money generated was delivered to the Contras in Nicaragua in order to finance their insurgency against a socialist regime there, which the Reagan administration could not abide. Congress had been expressly forbidden any actions in favor of the Contras. When exposed, the Iran/Contra scandal nearly brought down the Reagan administration. A detailed analysis of this can be found in Theodore Draper's excellent book, *A Very Thin Line*.

Iraq's war against Iran came to an end after a cease fire was signed in 1988. The war had devastated the Iraqi economy, motivating Hussein to announce a $40 billion program to peacefully rebuild his nation.

This proved impossible; the other Gulf states had been dumping oil onto the world markets, intensely devaluing the price per barrel of petroleum. Saddam Hussein found himself in crushing debt, but with the largest army in the region. The United States, worried that its ally of so many years might turn on his neighbors, redrafted War Plan 1002 in 1989. Originally designed to counter a Soviet threat, War Plan 1002 became 1002-90, officially designating Iraq as the main threat in the region. In 1990, America warned Baghdad against any provocative actions against its neighbors. Primary among American concerns was the possibility of an Iraqi attack on Israel.

These warnings went unheeded. In May of 1990, Saddam Hussein accused the other gulf states of waging economic war against Iraq. The debt Hussein had amassed in his war with Iran had become a threat to the existence of his nation, motivating him to desperate action. Hussein accused Kuwait of plotting to destroy the Iraqi economy by slant-drilling for oil into Iraqi territory. Hussein claimed that Kuwait was in fact a province of Iraq, and not a separate nation in and of itself. Iraqi troops massed on the Kuwaiti border and on August 2, 1990, Saddam Hussein's armies invaded Kuwait, drastically altering the balance of petroleum power in the region, and threatening American access to oil.

On August 3, 1990, the United Nations passed resolution 660, condemning Iraq for the invasion of Kuwait. On August 6, the U.N. passed resolution 661, levying economic sanctions against Iraq in order to compel them to leave Kuwait. This was a devastating blow. Iraq imported 70% of its food. By September,

Iraq was forced to begin food rationing. By December, the infant mortality rate in Iraq had doubled. Still, Hussein refused to withdraw from Kuwait.

By November of 1990, some 400,000 troops from an international coalition formed by President George Herbert Walker Bush were in the region. The majority of these troops were based in Saudi Arabia, home to the sacred Islamic sites of Mecca and Medina. The arrival of these troops in Saudi Arabia infuriated a wealthy Saudi named Osama bin Laden, who had made a name for himself while fighting against the Soviet invasion of Afghanistan. As America steeled itself to attack one threat, it gave birth to another.

On January 9, America threatened Iraq with destruction if it did not leave Kuwait. Three days later, Congress authorized the use of force against Iraq. Five days later, the international coalition began a dizzying and deadly aerial assault upon Iraqi forces. For forty-two days they bombed and strafed, sending 2,000 sorties a day against the Iraqi armies and air force. After a month of this punishing assault, President Bush urged the Iraqi people to rise up against Saddam Hussein, who Bush had publicly compared to Adolf Hitler. No such popular uprising took place.

On February 23, the ground assault against Iraq began. Ravaged by the air campaign, Iraqi forces fell apart almost immediately, and within three days Iraq announced its withdrawal from Kuwait. On February 28, Iraq and the United States agreed to a cease-fire. The Gulf War was over.

The fighting, however, was not. On March 2,

1991, thousands of Iraqi soldiers were destroyed by the American 24th Mechanized Infantry. Meanwhile, Saddam Hussein remained in power. U.S.-encouraged rebellions against Hussein were foiled. Commanding General Norman Schwartzkopf allowed Iraqi helicopters to fly across U.S. lines to attack and destroy rebelling Shiites and Kurds in the north and south, but then refused to allow Republican Guard units – who had risen up against Hussein – to reach their stores of weapons. Hussein viciously crushed these insurgents, further solidifying his rule. The United States had fought a war to remove Hussein from Kuwait, but made sure in the war's aftermath that Hussein would remain in control. Soon after the end of the war, Saddam Hussein declared victory over the United States.

In the aftermath of the war, the economic sanctions against Iraq were held in place. Over a million Iraqi civilians have died since as the direct result of the deprivations created by these sanctions. The United Nations Security Council passed resolution 687 in April of 1991, creating the weapons of mass destruction inspection teams that went under the name UNSCOM. President Bush was defeated in the elections of 1992 by William Jefferson Clinton, who continued the Bush policy of containing Iraq. From the end of the Gulf War until today, pinprick attacks by American combat aircraft against Iraqi air defense installations became so regular a practice that they were rarely reported by the American media. Inspection teams methodically located and destroyed all aspects of Iraq's chemical, nuclear, and biological programs until 1998, when a manufactured crisis heralded the

removal of the inspection teams by UNSCOM head
Richard Butler. The details of this are described in
depth in the following interview.

AN INTERVIEW WITH SCOTT RITTER

"The first panacea for a mismanaged nation is
inflation of the currency; the second is war.
Both bring a temporary prosperity; both bring a
permanent ruin. But both are the refuge of
political and economic opportunists."

Ernest Hemingway

*The following interview took place via telephone over the
course of several hours on August 16th and 19th, 2002.*

PITT: Considering your experience, and the time
you've spent in Iraq, does the United States have a
basis for war against that country?

RITTER: The United States can only have a basis for
war against Iraq if Iraq either attacks the United
States or is viewed by the international community –
in particular, the Security Council – as posing an inherent risk to international peace and security. Of
course if Iraq attacks the United States, then the
United States has the immediate right under Article 51
of the United Nations charter of self-defense to go to
war.

PITT: Does Iraq pose a risk to peace and security?

RITTER: This must be carefully considered by the Security Council. If the answer is deemed to be yes, a resolution under Chapter 7 of the United Nations charter would need to be passed.

A lot of people within the United States point to Chapter 7 resolutions that have already been passed by the Security Council as implying Iraq is a threat. In particular, they point to resolution 687, passed in April 1991, which creates UNSCOM, the weapons inspection organization; bans Iraq's weapons; and states that if Iraq doesn't comply, the United Nations has the option to use military force. I don't believe any international lawyers outside the United States believe resolution 687 gives the United States carte blanche to wage war against Iraq. That's something the Security Council would still need to deliberate on, and right now the Security Council hasn't provided any indication it supports the U.S. point of view – that existing conditions provide justification for war.

Right now the Bush Administration is pushing something called "The Right of Pre-Emptory Self-Defense." Here's how it works: If a nation expresses hostile intent and is accumulating the means to strike you, you're not obligated to sit back and wait for them to strike. You can find support for this in Article 51 of the United Nations Charter. According to this logic, the Allies could have pre-emptively attacked Germany, and perhaps saved millions of lives. It makes sense. Of course, this is precisely the excuse that Germany also used to attack Poland and many other countries. The reasoning is used frequently. Israel, for example, has used it on many occasions.

The hard part is determining hostile intent. How do you separate a real threat from a rationalization – including one you may yourself believe – that covers your own aggressive tendencies? At what point is a pre-emptive strike justified?

In Iraq's case, that question hinges around weapons of mass destruction, which have been outlawed in that country since 1991. Iraq has no right to retain them, and if they do have them now, more than ten years after these weapons were banned by the international community, clearly a case could be made that Iraq is manifesting ill intent. The United States would then have considerable support around the world for pre-emptive strikes against Iraq.

PITT: Does Iraq have weapons of mass destruction?

RITTER: It's not black-and-white, as some in the Bush administration make it appear. There's no doubt Iraq hasn't fully complied with its disarmament obligations as set forth by the Security Council in its resolution. But on the other hand, since 1998 Iraq has been fundamentally disarmed: 90–95% of Iraq's weapons of mass destruction capability has been verifiably eliminated. This includes all of the factories used to produce chemical, biological, and nuclear weapons, and long-range ballistic missiles; the associated equipment of these factories; and the vast majority of the products coming out of these factories.

Iraq was supposed to turn everything over to the

United Nations, which would supervise its destruction and removal. Iraq instead chose to destroy – unilaterally, without U.N. supervision – a great deal of
this equipment. We were later able to verify this. But
the problem is that this destruction took place without documentation, which means the question of
verification gets messy very quickly.

PITT: Why did Iraq destroy the weapons instead of
turning them over?

RITTER: In many cases the Iraqis were trying to con-
ceal the weapons' existence. And the unilateral destruction could have been a ruse to maintain a cache
of weapons of mass destruction by claiming they'd
been destroyed.

It's important to not give Iraq the benefit of the
doubt. Iraq has lied to the international community. It
has lied to inspectors. There are many people who believe Iraq still seeks to retain the capability to produce
these weapons.

That said, we have no evidence Iraq retains either
the capability or material. In fact, a considerable
amount of evidence suggests Iraq doesn't retain the
necessary material.

I believe the primary problem at this point is one
of accounting. Iraq has destroyed 90–95% of its
weapons of mass destruction. Okay. We have to remember that this missing 5–10% doesn't necessarily
constitute a threat. It doesn't even constitute a
weapons program. It constitutes bits and pieces of a
weapons program which in its totality doesn't
amount to much, but which is still prohibited. Like-

wise, just because we can't account for it doesn't mean Iraq retains it. There's no evidence Iraq retains this material. That's the quandary we're in. We can't give Iraq a clean bill of health, therefore we can't close the book on their weapons of mass destruction. But simultaneously we can't reasonably talk about Iraqi non-compliance as representing a de-facto retention of a prohibited capability worthy of war.

How do we deal with this uncertainty? There are those who say that because there are no weapons inspectors in Iraq today, because Iraq has shown a proclivity to acquire these weapons in the past and use these weapons against their neighbors and their own people, and because Iraq has lied to weapons inspectors in the past, we have to assume the worst. Under this rubric, a pre-emptive strike is justified.

If this were argued in a court of law, the weight of evidence would go the other way. Iraq has, in fact, demonstrated over and over a willingness to cooperate with weapons inspectors. Mitigating circumstances surround the demise of inspections and the inconclusive or incomplete nature of the mission, by which I mean Iraq's failure to be certified as fully disarmed. Those seeking to implement these resolutions – for example, the United States – actually violated the terms of the resolutions by using their unique access to operate inside Iraq in a manner incompatible with Security Council resolutions, for example, by spying on Iraq.

PITT: Five things generally draw the attention of the U.S. government and the people interested in attacking Iraq. They are: 1) the potential for nuclear weapons; 2) the potential for chemical weapons; 3) the potential for biological weapons; 4) the potential for delivery systems that could reach the United States; and 5) possible connections between Saddam Hussein and Al Qaeda or other terrorist networks. I'd like to talk for a moment about Iraq's nuclear weapons program.

RITTER: When I left Iraq in 1998, when the U.N. inspection program ended, the infrastructure and facilities had been 100% eliminated. There's no debate about that. All of their instruments and facilities had been destroyed. The weapons design facility had been destroyed. The production equipment had been hunted down and destroyed. And we had in place means to monitor – both from vehicles and from the air – the gamma rays that accompany attempts to enrich uranium or plutonium. We never found anything. We can say unequivocally that the industrial infrastructure needed by Iraq to produce nuclear weapons had been eliminated.

Even this, however, is not simple, because Iraq still had thousands of scientists who'd been dedicated to this nuclear weaponization effort. The scientists were organized in a very specific manner, with different sub-elements focused on different technologies of interest. Even though the physical infrastructure had been eliminated, the Iraqis chose to retain the organizational structure of the scientists. This means Iraq has thousands of nuclear scientists – along with their knowledge and expertise – still organized in the same manner as when Iraq had a nuclear weapons program and its accompanying infrastructure. Those scientists are today involved in legitimate tasks. These jobs aren't illegal per se, but they do allow these scientists to continue working in fields similar to those in which they'd work were they in fact carrying out a nuclear weapons program.

There is concern, then, that the Iraqis might intend in the long run to re-establish or reconstitute a nuclear weapons program. But this concern must be tempered by reality. That's not something that could happen overnight, nor is it something that could happen as long as weapons inspectors were inside Iraq. For Iraq to reacquire nuclear weapons capability, they'd have to basically build, from the ground up, enrichment and weaponization capabilities that would cost tens of billions of dollars. Nuclear weapons cannot be created in a basement or cave. They require modern industrial infrastructures that in turn require massive amounts of electricity and highly controlled technologies not readily available on the open market.

PITT: Like neutron reflectors, tampers ...

RITTER: Iraq could design and build these itself. I'm talking more about flash cameras and the centrifuges needed to enrich uranium. There are also specific chemicals required. None of this can be done on the cheap. It's very expensive, and readily detectable.

The Vice President has been saying that Iraq might be two years away from building a nuclear bomb. Unless he knows something we don't, that's nonsense. And it doesn't appear he does, because whenever you press the Vice President or other Bush administration officials on these claims, they fall back on testimony by Richard Butler, my former boss, an Australian diplomat, and Khidir Hamza, an Iraqi defector who claims to be Saddam's bomb-maker. And of course that's not good enough, especially when we have the United Nations record of Iraqi disarmament from 1991 to 1998. That record is without dispute. It's documented. We eliminated the nuclear program, and for Iraq to have reconstituted it would require undertaking activities eminently detectable by intelligence services.

PITT: Because these claims by the Vice President are so important to the debate, I want to be clear. Are you saying that Iraq could not hide, for example, gas centrifuge facilities, because of the energy the facilities would require and the heat they would emit?

RITTER: It's not just heat. Centrifuge facilities emit gamma radiation, as well as many other frequencies. It's detectable. Iraq could not get around this.

PITT: What about chemical weapons?

RITTER: Iraq manufactured three kinds of nerve agents: Sarin, Tabun, and VX. Some people who want war with Iraq describe 20,000 munitions filled with Sarin and Tabun nerve agents that could be used against Americans. The facts, however, don't support this. Sarin and Tabun have a shelf life of five years. Even if Iraq had somehow managed to hide this vast number of weapons from inspectors, what they're now storing is nothing more than useless, harmless goo.

Chemical weapons were produced in the

Muthanna State establishment: a massive chemical weapons factory. It was bombed during the Gulf War, and then weapons inspectors came and completed the task of eliminating the facility. That means Iraq lost its Sarin and Tabun manufacturing base.

We destroyed thousands of tons of chemical agent. It's not as though we said, "Oh we destroyed a factory, now we're going to wait for everything else to expire." We had an incineration plant operating full-time for years, burning tons of the stuff every day. We went out and blew up in place bombs, missiles, and warheads filled with this agent. We emptied SCUD missile warheads filled with this agent. We hunted down this stuff and destroyed it.

PITT: Couldn't the Iraqis have hidden some?

RITTER: That's a very real possibility. The problem is that whatever they diverted would have had to have been produced in the Muthanna State establishment, which means that once we blew it up, the Iraqis no longer had the ability to produce new agent, and in five years the Sarin and Tabun would have degraded and become useless sludge. It's no longer a viable chemical agent the world needs to be concerned about.

All this talk about Iraq having chemical weapons is no longer valid. Most of it is based on speculation that Iraq could have hidden some of these weapons from U.N. inspectors. I believe we did a good job of inspecting Iraq. Had they tried to hide it, we would have found it. But let's just say they did successfully hide some. So what? It's gone by now anyway. It's not even worth talking about.

PITT: Isn't VX gas a greater concern?

RITTER: VX is different, for a couple of reasons. First, unlike sarin and tabun, which the Iraqis admitted to, for the longest time the Iraqis denied they had a program to manufacture VX. Only through the hard work of inspectors were we able to uncover the existence of the program.

PITT: How did that happen?

RITTER: Inspectors went to the Muthanna State establishment and found the building the Iraqis had used for research and development. It had been bombed during the war, causing a giant concrete roof to collapse in on the lab. That was fortuitous, because it meant we essentially had a time capsule: lifting the roof and gaining access to the lab gave us a snapshot of Iraqi VX production on the day in January when the bomb hit. We sent in a team who behaved like forensic archaeologists. They lifted the roof – courageously, it was a very dangerous operation – went inside, and were able to grab papers and take samples that showed that Iraq did in fact have a VX research and development lab.

Caught in that first lie, the Iraqis said, "We didn't declare the program because it never went anywhere. We were never able to stabilize the VX." Of course the inspectors didn't take their word for it, but pressed: "How much precursor did you build?" Precursor chemicals are what you combine to make VX. "How much VX did you make? Where did you dispose of it?" The Iraqis took the inspectors to a field where they'd dumped the chemicals. Inspectors took soil samples and indeed found degradation by-products of VX and its precursors.

Unfortunately, we didn't know whether they dumped all of it or held some behind. So we asked what containers they'd used. The Iraqis pointed to giant steel containers provided by the Soviet Union to ship fuel and other liquids, which the Iraqis had converted to hold VX. The inspectors attempted to do a swab on the inside of the containers and found they'd been bleached out: there was nothing there. But one inspector noticed a purge valve on the end of the containers. The inspection team took a swab and found stabilized VX.

We confronted the Iraqis with their second lie. They took a fallback position: "OK, you're right, we did stabilize VX. But we didn't tell you about it because we never weaponized the VX. To us it's still not a weapons program. We decided to eliminate it on our own. As you can see, we've blown it up. It's gone, so there's no need to talk about it."

We caught them in that lie as well. We found stabilized VX in SCUD missiles demolished at the warhead destruction sites. The Iraqis had weaponized the VX, and lied to us about it.

We knew the Iraqis wanted to build a full-scale VX nerve agent plant, and we had information that they'd actually acquired equipment to do this. We hunted and hunted, and finally in 1996 were able to track down two hundred crates of glass-lined production equipment Iraq had procured specifically for a VX nerve agent factory. They'd been hiding it from the inspectors. We found it in 1996, and destroyed it. With that, Iraq lost its ability to produce VX.

All of this highlights the complexity of these issues. We clearly still have an unresolved VX issue in
Iraq. Just as clearly Iraq has not behaved in a manner
reflective of an honest effort to achieve resolution.
And it's tough to work in a place where you've been
lied to. But when you step away from the emotion of
the lie and look at the evidence at hand, you see a destroyed research and development plant, destroyed
precursors, destroyed agent, destroyed weapons, and
a destroyed factory.

That's pretty darned good. Even if Iraq had held
on to stabilized VX agent, it's likely it would have degraded by today. Real questions exist as to whether
Iraq perfected the stabilization process. Even a minor
deviation in the formula creates proteins that destroy
the VX within months. The real question is: Is there a
VX nerve agent factory in Iraq today? Not on your
life.

PITT: Could those facilities have been rebuilt?

RITTER: No weapons inspection team has set foot in
Iraq since 1998. I think Iraq was technically capable of
restarting its weapons manufacturing capabilities
within six months of our departure. That leaves three
and one half years for Iraq to have manufactured and
weaponized all the horrors the Bush Administration
claims as motivations for the attack. The important
phrase here, however, is "technically capable." If no
one were watching, Iraq could do this. But just as with
the nuclear weapons program, they'd have to start
from scratch, having been deprived of all equipment,
facilities and research. They'd have to procure the com-

plicated tools and technology required through front companies. This would be detected. The manufacture of chemical weapons emits vented gases that would have been detected by now if they existed. We've been watching, via satellite and other means, and have seen none of this. If Iraq was producing weapons today, we'd have definitive proof, plain and simple.

PITT: You're sure the inspections programs didn't miss anything.

RITTER: From 1994 to 1998 we had monitoring inspectors blanketing the totality of Iraq's chemical industrial facilities, installing sensitive sniffers and cameras, and performing no-notice inspections. We detected no evidence of retained or reconstituted prohibited capability. We had mobile teams roaming Iraq with extremely sensitive detection equipment that shoots lasers across fields, then analyzes the particle content of air passing through the beams. Setting these up down-wind of chemical facilities enabled us to tell exactly what was being pumped out. Even though it wasn't our job, we were able to detect Iraqi air defense installations because the beams would detect nitric acid, an oxidizer used as the fuel for SCUD missiles. Tracing the source revealed Iraqi SA-2 air defense missile systems several kilometers away. It's extremely accurate stuff.

PITT: Do we have the ability to detect if Iraq attempts to reacquire equipment necessary to make chemical weapons?

RITTER: As a weapons inspector I worked with the intelligence communities of a number of nations to interdict Iraqi covert procurement efforts abroad. As we now know, the Iraqis have many covert procurement fronts in existence. Most of them deal with sanctions violations – getting the basic goods needed for day-to-day life and to keep their industrial infrastructure in place.

PITT: Are those the same sorts of covert fronts Halliburton – the company associated with Vice President Cheney – used when they were dealing with Iraq?

RITTER: Similar. I'd imagine, however, that the Halliburton fronts the Iraqis put up weren't run by intelligence services. But Iraqi intelligence services have covert procurement fronts around the world, many of them involved in buying conventional military equipment. Keep in mind that although it's not illegal for Iraq to have a conventional military, under sanctions Iraq isn't allowed to acquire any weapons or spare parts for their fleets of helicopters, aircraft, tanks, etc. Any military analyst will tell you that if you don't have spare parts pouring in, your fleet becomes rapidly not only outdated but inoperable.

PITT: I have a friend who drove tanks in the army. At least once a day he'd be up to his waist in mud trying to fix something.

RITTER: Tanks, airplanes, helicopters all eat up parts. So, part of the Iraqi covert procurement effort must be to acquire spare parts for their military. And they're doing that fairly successfully. That's why their air defense system is relatively formidable. That's why they can still operate tanks.

These covert fronts also acquire production equipment for legitimate civilian industries. By legitimate I don't mean they're allowable under the sanctions, but instead that they have nothing to do with the manufacture of weapons of mass destruction. Iraq is a modern industrial state. It needs machinery, and parts for machinery, in order to function. Economic sanctions deny them this, so the Iraqi intelligence service has to acquire it. That may be illegal, but our sole focus as inspectors was weapons of mass destruction.

I assembled lists of literally hundreds of Iraqi intelligence front companies operating around the world. We traveled everywhere investigating them. We never found concrete evidence of any involvement in acquiring proscribed items.

The closest we came was an Iraqi effort in Romania to buy a controlling interest in an aerospace company called Aerofina, with the goal of producing parts to be used to make the Al Samoud, a permitted missile with a range of less than 150 kilometers. Iraq was having problems indigenously producing parts for this missile, so they sought to acquire this capability abroad. Because this is a controlled technology, this action was illegal, a violation of the sanctions, and a violation of U.N. resolutions. Technically speaking, Iraq was in violation of the Security Council disarmament resolution. But that doesn't translate into a prohibited weapon, nor into what a reasonable person would consider an action necessitating attack.

PITT: And your investigations were thorough …

RITTER: We were very effective. Whenever an Iraqi delegation left Iraq, we got a tip off, found where they were going, who they were meeting with, what they were buying. We intercepted telexes and other communications. We bugged hotels. And we never found any evidence of them trying to acquire prohibited materials. In Iraq I led no-notice teams to these Iraqi front companies, scoured their documents. We found interesting things, such as evidence of at least sixty Frenchmen on the Iraqi payroll operating front companies in France. But when we investigated these companies, we found they had nothing to do with weapons of mass destruction. Our findings may have been of great interest to the French and others, but not to us.

Even with inspectors no longer operating inside Iraq, the capability exists, inherent in the intelligent services of other nations, to readily detect any effort by Iraq to acquire proscribed capabilities.

PITT: What about biological weapons?

RITTER: If you listen to Richard Butler, biological weapons are a 'black hole' about which we know nothing. But a review of the record reveals we actually know quite a bit. We monitored more biological facilities than any other category, inspecting over a thousand sites and repeatedly monitoring several hundred.

We found the same problem with biological weapons programs we found with VX: it took Iraq four years even to admit to having such a program. They denied it from 1991 to 1995, finally admitting it that summer.

PITT: What did they try to make?

RITTER: They didn't just try. They actually made it, primarily anthrax in liquid bulk agent form. They also produced a significant quantity of liquid botulinum toxin. They were able to weaponize both of these, put them in warheads and bombs. They lied about this capability for some time. When they finally admitted it in 1995 we got to work on destroying the factories and equipment that produced it.

Contrary to popular mythology, there's absolutely no evidence Iraq worked on smallpox, Ebola, or any other horrific nightmare weapons the media likes to talk about today.

The Al Hakum factory provides a case study of the difficulties we faced, and how we dealt with those difficulties. We'd known of this plant's existence since 1991, and had inspectors there who were very suspicious. Iraq declared it to be a single-cell protein manufacturing plant used to produce animal feed. That was ridiculous. No one produces animal feed that way. It would be the most expensive animal feed in the world. The place had high-quality fermentation and other processing units. We knew it was a weapons plant. The Iraqis denied it. Finally they admitted it, and we blew up the plant.

We theorized about the production rate of that plant, based on documentation about the growth media they'd used to nurture the anthrax. Iraq said it was for civilian use, but they had enough growth media to keep a civilian program going for centuries, and growth media has a shelf life of five to seven years. This and other circumstantial evidence suggested Iraq had planned on producing a whole bunch of anthrax. The inspectors requested production log books, which the Iraqis said didn't exist. Next, the Iraqis said the plant didn't operate at full capacity. Then they said they had limited production runs. A lot of inspectors didn't believe them. I'm not in a position to judge.

Iraq was able to produce liquid bulk anthrax. That is without dispute. Liquid bulk anthrax, even under ideal storage conditions, germinates in three years, becoming useless. So even if Iraq lied to us and held on to anthrax – and there's no evidence to substantiate this – it's pure theoretical speculation on the part of certain inspectors. Iraq has no biological weapons today, because both the anthrax and botulinum toxin are useless. For Iraq to have biological weapons today, they'd have to reconstitute a biological manufacturing base. And again, biological research and development was one of the things most heavily inspected by weapons inspectors. We blanketed Iraq – every research and development facility, every university, every school, every hospital, every beer factory: anything with a potential fermentation capability was inspected – and we never found any evidence of ongoing research and development or retention.

Testing has at times been misused. One example has to do with Dick Spertzel, who headed up U.N. biological inspection in the latter part of UNSCOM's time in Iraq. He's a former biological warfare officer for the U.S. Army, and played a role in U.S. biological offensive weapons manufacturing. So he's very knowledgeable. He stated that the U.N. would not do biological weapons sampling. One of the most egregious cases concerns the Iraqi presidential palaces. We went in there in 1998, in the midst of very strong rhetoric by many in the administration, for example Secretary of Defense Cohen, who held up a bag of sugar and said if it was anthrax it could kill Washington D.C. Many people were saying anthrax was being manufactured in Iraq's palaces. The world almost went to war to get us into them. Once we got in, we tested for nuclear and chemical weapons, and never found anything. But the biologists were prevented from conducting any tests. When the Iraqis confronted Dick Spertzel about this, he said he'd never expected biological weapons to be there, and hadn't wanted to give them the benefit of a negative reading.

PITT: It sounds like police detectives who refuse to put a search for a murder weapon in the search warrant, for fear of not being able to find it and then have to admit that into evidence.

RITTER: That's exactly what happened. It's ironic that Dick Spertzel has since complained that we have no information, and has also called Iraq's potential for biological weapons a black hole. It's absurd. The Iraqis repeatedly asked him to bring in sophisticated sensing equipment to test for biological weapons. He consistently said he wasn't going to carry out investigations that provide circumstantial evidence to support Iraq's contention they don't have these weapons.

PITT: It was certainly in the best interests of the Iraqis to allow the inspectors, because if a negative came back, they could continue to build a case for getting rid of the sanctions.

RITTER: I find it intellectually and morally incomprehensible that Richard Butler allowed Dick Spertzel to operate in this manner. On a number of occasions I got in near-shouting matches with Dick Spertzel during morning staff meetings about the way he was carrying out his investigation. I said over and over that it was one of the most unprofessional investigations I've ever seen. But he was in charge of biology. My job was to look for concealment. And I never found any evidence of concealment of biological weapons.

There's another story I want to tell you about our investigations of biological weapons systems. In September 1997 Diane Seaman, biologist and investigator extraordinaire, did a no-notice inspection of the Iraqi national standards laboratory, where they do food testing. She went in the back way, and ran into two gentlemen with briefcases coming down the stairs. They panicked when they saw her, and tried to run away. She chased them down, grabbed them, and seized the briefcases. She handed the briefcases to one of her subordinates, told him to get it out of there, then held off the Iraqis while the guy escaped with the briefcases.

In our headquarters, we opened the briefcases and saw they contained documentation from their Special Security Organization, Saddam's personal presidential security group. It's like the U.S. Secret Service, but much more brutal. I'd been investigating them for a while. Earlier we'd gotten a very detailed report that the Special Security Organization were using troops from Saddam's bodyguard unit to shuttle biological agent back and forth between certain facilities. When we investigated the report, we found it to accurately describe people and places. We took samples and never found any evidence of biological agent, but the SSO remained an organization we were concerned about. Now we suddenly had in our possession a briefcase belonging to the SSO, taken from guys trying to sneak out of the building. Even more incredible, the document letterhead said Special Biological Activity.

We were thinking we'd hit a home run. We rapidly began to translate – and I mean rapidly – and saw things like "botulinum toxin reagent test kits," and "clostridium perfingen reagent test kits." Both of these are agents developed by Iraq for weapons. We organized a meeting with the Iraqis, telling them we wanted to talk about this. The Iraqis refused, saying it had nothing to do with our work.

So we went to the headquarters of the Special Security Organization, which happened to be right near the presidential palace. We were stopped at gunpoint, threatened, and forced to terminate the inspection. This led to a major confrontation. The world got ready for war. But then we started a detailed translation of the document and found it wasn't about biological weapons at all, but about testing food: these are reports of the samples that people take of every piece of clothing, every bed linen, every piece of food, anything that comes into contact with the president and his inner circle. They have botulinum toxin reagent because botulinum toxin is a food poisoning. Same with the clostridium perfingen. The whole document, the "special biological activity," was about presidential security.

Truth matters little to how the story continues to be spun. This incident is still cited on national television and radio as an example of Iraq's continued work in biological weapons.

Just as with the nuclear and chemical weapons, there's a lot we don't know about Iraq's biological weapons capabilities. But there's also a lot we do. We know enough to say that as of December 1998 we had no evidence Iraq had retained biological weapons, nor that they were working on any. In fact, we had a lot of evidence to suggest Iraq was in compliance.

PITT: What about Iraq's delivery systems?

RITTER: Iraq is prohibited from having ballistic missiles with a range greater than 150 kilometers, but permitted to have missile systems with a lesser range. Iraq was actively working on two designs. One was a solid rocket motor design, and the other, the Al Samoud, uses liquid propulsion.

The propulsion system for the Al Samoud is basically an engine that burns as long as you give it fuel. Fuel tank size determines range. Iraq was developing a propulsion system that could easily be modified by lengthening the fuel tanks or clustering missiles together to increase range.

We monitored this project very closely, and found that the Iraqis have severe limitations on what they can produce within the country. Prior to the Gulf War Iraq acquired a lot of technology, as well as parts, from Germany, which has a record of precision machinery. After the war the Iraqis tried to replicate that, but with very little success. We watched them assemble their rockets, and because many of the members of our team were rocket scientists, we'd notice their mistakes. They had to show us their designs, and of course we didn't comment on them. But it quickly became apparent that the program was run by intelligent, energetic amateurs who were just not getting it right. They'd manufacture rockets that would spin and cartwheel, that would go north instead of south, that would blow up. Of course eventually they'd figure it out. But as of 1998 they were, according to optimistic estimates, five years away, even if sanctions were lifted and Iraq gained access to necessary technologies.

I often hear people talk about Iraq having multi-staging rockets. But Iraq doesn't have multi-staging capability. They tried that once, back in 1989 when the country had full access to this technology, and the rocket blew up in midair. I hear people talk about clustering, but Iraq tried that, too, and it didn't work. The bottom line is that Iraq doesn't have the capability to do long-range ballistic missiles. The don't even have the capability to do short-range ballistic missiles. They're trying, but not succeeding. I think we have to be concerned about this missile program, because the technologies are readily convertible, but the idea that Iraq can suddenly pop up with a long range missile is ludicrous. There's a lot of testing that has to take place, and this testing is all carried out outdoors. They can't avoid detection.

Of course now the inspectors have left Iraq, we

don't know what happens inside factories. But that doesn't really matter, since they can't conduct tests indoors. You have to bring rockets out, fire them on test stands. This is detectable. No one has detected any evidence of Iraq doing this. Iraq continues to declare its missile tests, normally around eight to twelve per year. Our radar detects the tests, we know what the characteristics are, and we know there's nothing to be worried about.

PITT: What about L-29s?

RITTER: For a while the CIA got the idea that L-29s, Czechoslovakian single-engine jets the Iraqis modified into drones – air defense targets – were being converted to deliver chemical and biological agents. In fact, there was a time when L-29s were dispersed to a variety of airfields, and the CIA became convinced they were getting ready to be launched as an attack against Turkey, Saudi Arabia, and others. I went to Israel and talked with the best experts in the Israeli Air Force, and their biologists. They were dismissive. They said it just doesn't make any sense – to deliver agent, you'd have to make modifications to the aircraft that are very specific and detectable. These modifications would also have an impact on range and fuel.

In any event, we got inspectors to the factory, and found no evidence of the Iraqis modifying L-29s along the lines the CIA suggested. It appeared to be a target drone program. Unfortunately, the CIA continues to this day to cite the L-29 as a potential delivery vehicle. They say that because inspectors aren't there, we have no way of knowing just what progress the

Iraqis have made. This is one of the things that could be readily cleared up once we get inspectors back inside Iraq.

PITT: This leaves the Al Qaeda connection to talk about.

RITTER: This one is patently absurd. Saddam is a secular dictator. He has spent the last thirty years declaring war against Islamic fundamentalism, crushing it. He fought a war against Iran in part because of Islamic fundamentalism. The Iraqis have laws on the books today that provide for an immediate death sentence for proselytizing in the name of Wahabbism, or indeed any Islam, but they are particularly virulent in their hatred of Wahabs, which is of course Osama bin Laden's religion. Osama bin Laden has a history of hating Saddam Hussein. He's called him an apostate, somebody who needs to be killed.

PITT: Even Osama bin Laden uses sanctions against Iraq as a rallying cry.

RITTER: Because American sanctions don't target Saddam. They target Iraqi civilians.

There has never been a link between Osama bin Laden and Saddam Hussein. Even the alleged meeting we heard so much about that was supposed to take place in Prague, Czechoslovakia. Intelligence services today say it's highly unlikely the meeting took place. Considerable evidence suggests Mohammed Atta was in Florida at that time.

Iraqi defectors have been talking lately about the

training camp at Salman Pak, south of Baghdad. They say there's a Boeing aircraft there. That's not true. There's an Antonov aircraft of Russian manufacture. They say there are railroad mock-ups, bus mock-ups, buildings, and so on. These are all things you'd find in a hostage rescue training camp, which is what this camp was when it was built in the mid-1980s with British intelligence supervision. In fact, British SAS special operations forces were sent to help train the Iraqis in hostage rescue techniques. Any nation with a national airline and that is under attack from terrorists – and Iraq was, from Iran and Syria at the time – would need this capability. Iraq operated Salman Pak as a hostage rescue training facility up until 1992. In 1992, because Iraq no longer had a functioning airline, and because their railroad system was inoperative, Iraq turned the facility over to the Iraqi Intelligence service, particularly the Department of External Threats. These are documented facts coming out of multiple sources from a variety of different countries. The Department of External Threats was created to deal with Kurdistan, in particular, the infusion of Islamic fundamentalist elements from Iran into Kurdistan. So, rather than being a camp dedicated to train Islamic fundamentalist terrorists, it was a camp dedicated to train Iraq to deal with Islamic fundamentalist terrorists.

And they did so. Their number one target was the Islamic Kurdish party, which later grew into Al Ansar. Now, Jeff Goldberg claimed in the *New Yorker* that Al Ansar is funded by the Iraqi Intelligence service. But that's exactly the opposite of reality: the Iraqis have been fighting Al Ansar for years now. Ansar comes out of Iran and is supported by Iranians. Iraq, as part of their ongoing war against Islamic fundamentalism, created a unit specifically designed to destroy these people.

It would be ludicrous for Iraq to support Al Qaeda, either conventionally, as many have claimed, or even worse, to give it weapons of mass destruction …

PITT: Because Al Qaeda might turn around and use them against Hussein.

RITTER: Not *might*. Would! Saddam is the apostate, the devil incarnate. He's evil in the eyes of these people.

There are no facts to back up claimed connections between Iraq and Al Qaeda. Iraq has no history of dealing with terrorists of this nature. It does have a history of using terrorism as a tool, but it's been used by Iraqi terrorists primarily focused on Iran, Syria, and Iraqi opposition members abroad.

PITT: Let's talk about the "bomb-making defector."

RITTER: Khidir Hamza.

PITT: Who is he?

RITTER: He claims to be Saddam's bomb-maker, responsible for the design of the Iraqi nuclear weapon and the brain behind the whole nuclear program. Unfortunately, a lot of people believe him. He testified before the U.S. Senate recently, and no one challenged his credentials. He repeatedly gets on American television.

The reality is that he was involved with the Iraqi nuclear program back in the mid-1980s as a mid-level functionary. He used to work with Hussein Kamal, Saddam Hussein's son-in-law, who ran the military industrial commission and used it not only to produce weapons of mass destruction for the president but also to enrich himself. Hamza didn't design nuclear weapons. He might, on occasion, have provided Hussein Kamal with the ability to review documents coming in from nuclear weapons designers to see if they were lying, and he also reviewed documents to see if the procurement requirements were legitimate.

Hamza finally was fired. He defected in 1994, and the CIA rejected him – the entire intelligence community rejected him – because they knew he wasn't who he said he was. Keep in mind that the CIA had very good defectors from the nuclear weapons program who left in 1991 who had been able to help the CIA identify the totality of the nuclear weapons program and help lead UNSCOM to capturing nuclear archives, including all the personnel records, all the operational design work, and so on. He wasn't a designer, and he certainly he wasn't the head of the program. The head of the program was Jafar al Jafar.

Investigating Iraq's nuclear program and how the country may be concealing it was one of my prime responsibilities. I've interviewed all of the primary people who worked on it, from Jafar al Jafar on down. I worked very closely with the International Atomic Energy Agency to review all documentation. Hamza is not who he says he is. Yet he has been embraced by the American media.

PITT: What about Hamza's "smoking gun" document showing that Iraq was developing a nuclear bomb?

RITTER: Hussein Kamal defected in 1995. When we showed him the document, he immediately said it was a forgery, and pointed out everything that was wrong with it. And remember that when Hussein Kamal defected, part of his purpose was to overthrow Saddam Hussein. He wanted to hurt Saddam's credibility, so it was not in his interest to pan a document that would help generate international support to take out Saddam's regime. But he couldn't support something he saw as a crude forgery.

Again and again I have offered to debate Khidir Hamza. He refuses to appear with me. He's scared of me, because he knows I've got a file that exposes the facts.

PITT: Another person you've challenged to debate is Richard Butler.

RITTER: I have a standing invitation for Richard Butler. I'll debate him anytime, anyplace.

PITT: Who is Butler?

RITTER: He's an Australian diplomat who comes from a political background. He was heavily involved in Australian politics, and parlayed that political involvement into a diplomatic career that touched upon arms control. He spent time in Vienna as Australia's ambassador to the International

Atomic Energy Agency. He played a role in the non-proliferation treaty. As the Australian ambassador to the United Nations, he has continued to dabble in arms control. He's very telegenic, very well-spoken, highly educated. So, when Rolf Ekeus, the first head of UNSCOM from 1991 to June of 1997, resigned, Richard Butler was tapped by the Secretary General to come in and take Ekeus's place.

PITT: And Butler now says publicly you don't know what you're talking about …

RITTER: He doesn't agree with what I'm saying. The problem for Richard is that I can document everything I say. Because of the politics of the time, it's convenient to have someone like Richard Butler, with his resume, on national TV blasting Saddam.

I've repeatedly challenged Richard Butler to debate me in front of a camera and a live audience. He won't do it. He's avoiding the kind of debate he should be encouraging.

I put Butler in a slightly different category than Hamza. I think Butler believes what he's saying, and is convinced he can dispel what I've been saying. But he can't.

PITT: What is Butler's motivation for this?

RITTER: Remember, Richard Butler is the equivalent of a Navy Captain of an aircraft carrier when it ran aground. UNSCOM no longer functions because of Richard Butler. So he's doing everything he can to give himself a more positive legacy.

PITT: How was UNSCOM run into the ground? Wasn't it infiltrated by the CIA?

RITTER: I don't know if I'd call it infiltration. There was certainly CIA involvement, a lot of which was legitimate. But the question becomes: who's calling the shots? It's one thing to build a team that incorporates CIA elements, which I did all the time – every one of my teams had CIA members in it. I needed them. They're good. They provided tremendous capabilities required if you're going to take on the Iraqis in the game I was playing.

As long as all of the activities inside Iraq are consistent with the U.N. mandate – looking for weapons of mass destruction – you don't have a problem. The second you start allowing inspections to be used to gather intelligence information unrelated to the mandate, you've discredited the entire inspection regime. Several programs – most importantly, a signals intelligence program I designed and ran from 1996 to 1998 – were allowed to be taken over by the CIA for the sole purpose of spying on Saddam. This was wrong, and I said so on numerous occasions. The refusal to terminate that relationship was one of the main reasons I resigned in 1998.

PITT: Why were the UNSCOM inspectors pulled out in 1998?

RITTER: In August of that year a delegation went to Baghdad for discussions. The Iraqis were fed up with what they felt to be foot-dragging and deliberately provocations. They felt the inspectors were probing inappropriately into areas that dealt with the sovereignty and dignity of Iraq, and its national security. They wanted to clarify these issues. Richard Butler came in with a very aggressive program, and the Iraqis announced they weren't going to deal with him anymore. They felt he was no longer a fair and objective implementer of Security Council policy, that he was little more than a stooge for the U.S. Butler withdrew, and the Iraqis said they weren't going to deal with UNSCOM. This led to Richard Butler ordering the inspectors out in October.

Actually, the Iraqis had said from the beginning they weren't going to deal with American inspectors. Then they relented, but said they wouldn't let Americans do anything other than ongoing monitoring. At that point, Richard Butler pulled out all of the inspectors.

The U.S. prepared to bomb Iraq. The bombers were in the air. Then the Secretary General's office was able to get the Iraqis to agree to have the inspectors return without precondition, and the bombers were called back. But the Pentagon and White House felt they were being jerked around by the U.N., so a decision was made to bomb anyway. The bombing campaign had to coincide with inspection: the inspections were to be used as the trigger.

Inspectors were sent in to carry out sensitive inspections that had nothing to do with disarmament but had everything to do with provoking the Iraqis.

Iraq had already come up with a protocol for conducting what are called "sensitive site inspections," after several inspection teams I was involved in tried to get into special Republican Guard and other sensitive facilities around Baghdad. The Iraqis had said, reasonably enough, that they didn't want forty intelligence officers running around these sites. Rolf Ekeus flew to Iraq in June of 1996 and worked out an agreement called the "Modalities for Sensitive Site Inspections." When inspectors came to a site that the Iraqis declared to be sensitive, the Iraqis had to facilitate the immediate entry of a four-man inspection element that would ascertain whether this site had anything to do with weapons of mass destruction, or whether it was indeed sensitive. If it was sensitive, the inspection was over.

These Sensitive Site modalities were accepted by the Security Council, and became part and parcel of the framework of the operating instructions. And they worked, not perfectly, but well enough to enable us to do our jobs from 1996 to 1998.

Directions were given that when the inspectors went in to Iraq that December, they were to make null and void the Sensitive Site modalities. This was done without coordinating with the Security Council. The only nation coordinated with was the United States.

The inspectors went in to Iraq, and to a Ba'ath Party headquarters in downtown Baghdad. The Iraqis said it was a sensitive site but the four-person team was welcome to come in. The inspectors unilaterally made null and void the Sensitive Site modalities, and said the entire inspection team was going to come in. The Iraqis compromised by allowing a six-man element to inspect. The element found nothing. Still the chief inspector demanded a much larger team be given access. The Iraqis responded that only under the Sensitive Site modalities would they allow a team back in. The inspectors withdrew and reported to Richard Butler. Butler cited this as an egregious violation of the Security Council mandate.

The inspection teams were withdrawn in direct violation of a promise to the other members of the Security Council: that inspectors would not be withdrawn without going through the Security Council to inform them and get their permission. The inspectors work for the Council. Two days later the bombing campaign started, using Richard Butler's report to the Security Council as justification – his report saying, of course, that the inspectors weren't being allowed to do their jobs by the Iraqis.

PITT: All of this will make it very difficult to get American inspectors back inside Iraq.

RITTER: This will make it difficult to get any inspectors back in. The Iraqis will need to be guaranteed inspectors won't again be used in such a non-sanctioned manner.

PITT: Those who want to go to war with Iraq often talk about "bringing democracy to Iraq." Could you talk about that?

RITTER: It's ludicrous for Donald Rumsfeld and others to talk about democracy in Iraq. The western democratic model is based on majority rule. But in Iraq, 60% of the population are Shi'a Muslims, theocratically aligned with Iran. Iran is, of course, a hotbed of anti-American Islamic fundamentalism.

Iraq is a nation with the second-largest proven reserves of oil. The idea of a democracy in Iraq where the Shi'a take control – meaning that these two large oil producers are theocratically aligned – is something not many people want. Not many in the region would support that. We really don't want democracy in Iraq, because we don't want the Shi'a to have control.

The second largest group is the Kurds, around 23% of the population. And the truth is that we don't want the Kurds to have independence anymore than the Turks do. And the Turks have been fighting a long and bloody war to prevent an independent Kurdistan. The United States has no interest in democratically empowering that 23% of the population.

This means we're really talking about the remaining 17%: the Sunnis. Saddam is a Sunni. The Sunni tribes have always dominated Iraqi politics. They've dominated the military, they've dominated the governing class. But even amongst the Sunnis we're not talking about democracy.

PITT: You've described Sunni governance in terms of the movie *The Godfather*.

RITTER: There's a scene where Don Corleone calls the Families together. If you walked in on that scene, you'd say, "My God, these Italian families get along famously." The reality is they don't. They war against each other, they connive, they lie, they steal, they dissolve and remake alliances until one family emerges dominant.

That's what has happened in Iraq. Saddam Hussein's family, the Abu Nassir, are 20,000 strong and control a nation of over 20 million. They do it because their family has emerged dominant, they can dominate the Sunnis. And then the Sunnis in turn dominate the Kurds and the Shi'a.

That's the reality. If you replace Saddam Hussein, it's probably going to be with another Sunni, which means the Sunni tribal hierarchy will kick in and you'll end up with a regime that rules in same manner as Saddam Hussein's.

It's all absurd anyway. You can't impose democracy from the outside. That doesn't work. Iraq has to make that transition internally, and that takes decades. The only way that can happen, the only way there can be a birth of democracy, is to lift economic sanctions and allow Iraq to reconstruct itself economically. The development of a viable middle class that cuts across religious, ethnic, and tribal lines is the only thing that can give birth to democracy.

PITT: When the United States went into Afghanistan, it used the Northern Alliance as proxy warriors, fighters on the ground. There's been a lot of talk about using the Kurds similarly if the U.S. invades Iraq. Is that a viable option?

RITTER: No. First, the Kurds war among themselves, too much in-fighting. Second, the Turks would never allow the Kurds to achieve that kind of dominance. Third, the Kurds themselves don't seem too keen on this role. Recently there was a meeting in Washington D.C. of all the Iraqi opposition groups. The largest Kurdish group in Iraq, the Kurdish Democratic Party, boycotted it. They said, "What guarantees can you give us? When you start building up for war, Saddam's not going to sit there. He's going to lash out, and he's going to lash out at Kurdistan. He'll crush us. What will you do to stop it? You can't do anything to stop it, because you're building up to take him out. If you intervene to keep him from crushing us, you divert your resources. This is a lose-lose situation for the Kurds, so we're not participating."

PITT: What will be the tactical situation if the U.S. goes to war in Iraq? Who can the U.S. count on as allies? What bases can they use?

RITTER: I believe Turkey would allow us to use bases if we promise to secure Kurdistan and prevent the Kurds from declaring independence. I think that will be one of the first steps you'll see, and relatively soon. We already have U.S. forces in Kurdistan expanding airfields and building up logistics bases. Sometime this fall we'll probably see the deployment of several thousand American troops in Kurdistan, ostensibly to protect the Kurds from Iraq as part of an extension of the no-fly zone/safe haven concept. That action will be to buy Turkish cooperation.

The main thrust will come from the south, out of Kuwait. It will be supported by American logistics and air bases that have been developed in Qatar, the United Arab Emirates and Bahrain, and will involve anywhere from 70,000 to 150,000 troops. The thrust will be designed to seize southern Iraq, install the Iraqi opposition, and then begin a drive on Baghdad in the hope that the Iraqi army will disintegrate and the people of Iraq, and especially of Baghdad, will rise up and overthrow Saddam. We'll also run a significant special operations war out of Jordan into western Iraq to keep Iraq from firing missiles into Israel, which would in turn prompt an Israeli response that could fracture this whole coalition. But the main thrust will come from the south.

PITT: What will be the response by other nations in the region?

RITTER: First, there's is a good chance this whole military campaign will fail, because it has so many built-in assumptions: a) the Iraqi army won't fight; b) The Iraqi population will rise up; and c) once we demonstrate our seriousness about removing Saddam, the international community will rally around us.

PITT: To date, the international community has been less than enthusiastic.

RITTER: They're galvanizing against it. There's tremendous resentment in the Arab world right now. If America engages in a unilateral invasion of Iraq, we …

PITT: Brent Scowcroft recently described it as *Armageddon*.

RITTER: It could get that way. There's a real potential for that. We'll be racing two factors: time and casualties. If we go into Iraq, we're going to have to win quickly. We aren't going to have the latitude for a long, drawn-out campaign. If the Iraqis can delay our action for any amount of time – a month, two, if Saddam can hang on – the Arab world will explode in a way we've never seen, a way that will make 9/11 look like a kid's game.

And if we suffer casualties, we're going to have a political disaster here in the United States. When you combine international condemnation with a disgruntled American populace, the President is going to be deeply embattled.

PITT: Particularly in the international community, if we don't secure some sort of U.N. mandate ...

RITTER: That will never happen. We'll claim we already have one, but we don't, and this could be the death of the U.N.'s viability as a promoter of peace and security.

PITT: Which might suit the purposes of some within this administration.

RITTER: The irony is that when you say there's a chance Egypt, Jordan, Saudi Arabia could fall, the Bush Administration says, "So what?" They've been saying all along there has to be a realignment in the Middle East, that the Middle East is out of touch with Western-oriented societies.

This is truly becoming the clash of cultures Osama bin Laden wanted. That's one reason he attacked us: He wanted to turn this into a war between the West and Islam. Almost everyone said that's ridiculous. But the *United States* is turning this into a war between the West and Islam. And we won't win. It's not that we'll suddenly be occupied, but we'll lose by not winning. It could be a humiliating defeat for the United States, a significant defeat that could mean the beginning of the retrograde of American influence around the world. It could be devastating to our economy.

It unleashes some very dangerous potential. Read the Nuclear Policy Review planning document put out by the Pentagon. Though they say it's just hypothetical, one of the scenarios concerns tens of thousands of American troops bogged down in a war overseas at risk not only of being eliminated, but at risk of weapons of mass destruction. We've already assumed an Iraqi chemical and biological capability. They may not possess it, but in all of our planning scenarios we give it to them. If 70,000 to 100,000 troops get bogged down in Iraq, and the Middle East explodes, threatening our lines of communication, threatening our ability to support these troops, and the Iraqis resist, the potential for nuclear release is very real.

That's where Armageddon comes in. No one today can ever envision giving terrorists a nuclear weapon; it would be very difficult for them to acquire one. But if either the United States or Israel were to use a nuke against Iraq, I guarantee within ten years the United States would be struck by a terrorist nuclear bomb. And then all bets will be off. If the U.S. or Israel used nukes against Iraq, Pakistan and Iran would turn over nuclear capability to terrorists. I guarantee this. There's Armageddon. This war with Iraq is the dumbest thing I've ever heard of.

AN INTERVIEW WITH SCOTT RITTER

PITT: What would be the immediate human cost of a war in Iraq?

RITTER: Iraq won't roll over. I don't believe the Iraqi people will rise against Saddam, or if they do, they'll be brutally repressed. I think if the U.S. makes a move in the south, Saddam will crack down on the Shi'a, and that will result in 20,000 to 30,000 being killed. Saddam will preemptively strike Kurdistan, killing 10,000 to 20,000 Kurds. The United States will have to "reduce" Baghdad, an urban area with 5 million people. Just think Grozny, when the Russians went after the Chechens. This will be even worse, and we'll kill 30,000 to 40,000 civilians. We're talking about a tremendous number of civilian casualties, not to mention the tens of thousands of Iraqi soldiers and security personnel who will perish.

PITT: You've described the American military as the greatest killing machine in history.

RITTER: We can kill more efficiently than anyone else in the world. The question is, what will constrain us? When you start talking about urban warfare and digging people out of a built-up area loaded with civilians, your options are very limited as to what you can do. Understand that we will also take considerable casualties. Our death toll will be in the high hundreds, if not thousands.

PITT: And in the worst-case scenario …

RITTER: If the whole situation collapses and we have

70,000 Americans cut off in Iraq facing the prospect of annihilation, we'll nuke. There's no doubt about it. We'll nuke. This is a war that has everything bad about it. There's no good end for this war.

PITT: Who in the American government is driving this push for war? You've heard recent comments by Condoleeza Rice seeming to lay out only two options: do nothing or go to war.

RITTER: Condoleeza Rice isn't a player.

PITT: She's a mouthpiece. But for whom?

RITTER: Donald Rumsfeld, Paul Wolfowitz and Richard Perle.

PITT: Why?

RITTER: Because they come from a neo-conservative think-tank environment that has extremely close ties to Israel, and which views Iraq as a threat to Israel and the United States. They've committed themselves ideologically, intellectually, politically, to Saddam Hussein's removal.

PITT: You think Israel is the pivot here?

RITTER: No. Leave Israel out of it. Israel isn't driving this. I'm saying that these are neo-conservatives with a very pro-Israel slant. Some of Israel's worst enemies are pro-Israeli Americans. I view Donald Rumsfeld and Paul Wolfowitz as among the worst enemies of

Israel today. I consider myself very pro-Israel, and if you care about Israel, this policy of a unilateral strike against Iraq is the worst thing possible. It destabilizes the Middle East even further, and puts Israel more at risk. It's just bad policy.

PITT: How would you define neo-conservative? I ask because I know you're a Republican who supported Bush in 2000.

RITTER: I'd define neo-conservatives as those who reject anything outside their ideological framework. I believe conservatives can listen to moderates and at least consider other viewpoints. But neo-conservatives are so committed to their ideology they won't consider anything else. In the case of Iraq, neo-conservatives are those who, in the past decade, have operated in certain think-tanks – the American Enterprise Institute comes to mind – where they've developed what is, to be honest, a fringe viewpoint on Iraq.

After Bush failed to get the mandate he needed in the election to reach out and bring in Democrats and more moderate voices, he had to fall back on his neo-conservative base, which suddenly empowered these fringe thinkers. These people are definitely not representative of mainstream thinking here in America.

They now have their hands on the reins of government …

PITT: And the military …

RITTER: Especially the Pentagon. Donald Rumsfeld was politically dead. No one thought of Donald

Rumsfeld as having any potential. Paul Wolfowitz was seen as a raving lunatic of the far right. Richard Perle is not called "The Prince of Darkness" without cause. These are three people who seemed destined to spend the rest of their political lives sniping from the fringes, as they'd done for the previous decade. And now, suddenly, they're running the show.

PITT: Pretty dangerous times.

RITTER: Extremely dangerous.

PITT: You think oil doesn't have very much to do with this.

RITTER: No. Oil is everywhere in that part of the world. We can get all the oil we want from Iraq. The Iraqi Oil Minister has made it clear that, once the sanctions are lifted, Iraq will do whatever they can to ensure the strategic energy requirements of the United States are met. It's not that Iraq is denying us access to oil.

PITT: What did you think about the recent Senate Foreign Relations Committee hearings – the Biden hearings – regarding this potential conflict?

RITTER: I've long encouraged the Senate to hold hearings on Iraq, and I traveled to Washington DC in June to meet with a number of Senators and their staffs. I tried to have a meeting with Joe Biden and his staff, but they refused to return my calls. I was told by the senior staffers in Chuck Hagel's and John Kerry's offices that Biden didn't want to talk about hearings: it wasn't on his agenda. Obviously something changed between June and the end of July, and the hearings were held. But they weren't fair and objective.

Instead, it was a kangaroo court, a sham, where the Senators brought together a hand-picked panel, including Butler and Hamza, pre-ordained to find that Iraq was a threat.

It's all very strange. When Joe Biden announced these hearings on Fox News Sunday – which in itself speaks volumes – in the same breath that he praised American democracy and talked about the need for debate and dialogue, he said that if Saddam is here in five years, we've made a mistake. He said he was confident that after the hearings he'd be able to get a near-unanimous decision from Congress authorizing military force against Iraq. If that's not a foregone conclusion, I don't know what is.

PITT: They talked about "regime change," but not about the process, the war.

RITTER: That's all they talked about. If Biden and the senators were judges, and this was truly a debate about the threat posed by Iraq, they'd have to recuse themselves, because they're committed to regime change. They've invested so much political capital into regime change that it quickly becomes ludicrous to assume these senators would have anything resembling a fair and open hearing on Iraq, or the threat posed to the United States by Iraq.

PITT: Considering everything you've experienced,

how do you feel about the Iraqi government in general?

RITTER: The Iraqi government is firmly entrenched, having seen over thirty years of Ba'ath Party rule. The Ba'ath Party has seeped into every aspect of Iraqi life – cultural, economic, educational, political. It's irresponsible to oversimplify what's going on there, to try to somehow separate Saddam Hussein from the rest of the political machinery. It doesn't work that way.

I'm realistic in understanding that the Iraqi government is much stronger inside Iraq than most people give it credit for. I don't think people should take the Iraqi government too lightly. It's a brutal regime that has shown a disregard for international law and a definite disregard for human rights. It's a regime that has shown – as have many other governments around the world, including ours – an ability to lie to people about policy objectives. There's no need to beat around the Bush. The Iraqis failed to tell the truth. I understand this cannot be accepted. But in the world of politics, if you cut off all activity with those who tell lies, no one would be do business with anybody.

PITT: You've said that one of the most dangerous things that has happened in the United States is that Americans have allowed themselves to be lulled into a situation where 20 million Iraqi people – civilians going through their everyday lives – can be summed up by one guy, Saddam Hussein. When we talk about getting rid of him and his government, we miss the fact that we're also talking about 20 million ordinary people.

RITTER: Iraq isn't Saddam Hussein. He's a significant player, no doubt, but for us to personify a nation of more than twenty million people in one man is grotesquely ignorant.

PITT: How would you begin to approach the problem?

RITTER: The first thing I'd do is designate a special envoy – a representative of the United States government – and dispatch that person to Baghdad to sit and talk. And listen. Any solution that includes the military must include diplomacy. One of the reasons we can't get a coalition together is that we've forgone all aspects of diplomacy in dealing with Iraq. If Colin Powell can sit down with the North Korean foreign minister representative – North Korea being, of course, part of Bush's 'Axis of Evil' – we should be able to sit down with Iraq's.

Re-engaging diplomatically is important, because it begins the process of exchanging viewpoints. We can make clear our requirement that Iraq strictly adhere to the provisions of the Security Council resolution. We can also make clear – and I think this is vital – that we're willing to place disarmament ahead of regime removal. I think we're going to need a total re-evaluation of our policy goal objectives regarding Iraq. We cannot speak of disarmament and Iraq's obligation to the Security Council resolution requiring disarmament, and in the same breath speak of our desire to unilaterally and in violation of international law remove Saddam Hussein from power. This is especially true when we say that even if Iraq plays by the book, in terms of supporting inspectors, we're still going after Saddam. That's counterproductive in the extreme. Put disarmament ahead. Put international law ahead. Do everything you can to get weapons inspectors back inside Iraq.

PITT: What will it take to get inspectors back in?

RITTER: In the end, I believe Iraq has no choice but to accept, without precondition, the absolute requirement to get inspectors back in. That's the bottom line. But Iraq won't do that unless they have assurances the inspections won't again be abused – as they were in December 1998 by the United States – to provoke military action or collect intelligence on Saddam Hussein.

It's difficult to bring together concerns: the Security Council's legitimate requirement of no preconditions and absolute adherence and recognition that Iraq must abide by the provisions of the Security Council resolution on the one hand; and Iraq's legitimate concerns about its sovereignty and national security on the other.

That's where I think it would be helpful to have an honest broker step in. That would provide a confidence-building mechanism to allow these two concerns to be bridged. The honest broker would only operate if inspectors were allowed unfettered access without preconditions. Likewise, the broker will ensure there are no abuses. I believe if there had been an honest broker in December 1998, if the international community could have seen that the Iraqis were fully prepared to let inspectors into the Ba'ath Party site, Richard Butler would never have issued the report that he did, and the United States would not have been able to so callously disregard international law and go off to bomb Iraq in Operation Desert Fox.

I believe this kind of independent observer is an essential part of any future solution that focuses on getting inspectors back into Iraq.

PITT: You're a Marine Corps veteran, an officer, an intelligence officer. You spent seven years chasing down these weapons in Iraq to guarantee the safety and security of not only this country, but of that region and the world. Yet there are some in this country who call you a traitor for speaking about these things the way you do. How do you respond?

RITTER: People can say what they want, but I think the people who say that betray their ignorance. There's this little thing called the Constitution of the United States of America. When I put on the Marine Corps uniform and was charged with being an officer of the Marines, I took an oath to uphold and defend the Constitution against all enemies, foreign and domestic. That means I'm willing to lay down my life for that piece of paper and what it represents. That document speaks of we the people, and of a government of the people, by the people, for the people. It speaks of freedom of speech, individual civil liberties.

One of my favorite paintings is by Norman Rockwell. It says, "Freedom of Speech," and shows a town hall meeting in New England, with a gentleman standing up addressing the room. Older and younger generations look up at him. They don't have to agree with what he's saying, but he's speaking, making his voice heard. For me, the right of every citizen to speak embodies the principles of American democracy more than anything.

We're not a democracy unless citizens are involved. And I'm involved. People don't have to agree with me. I have no problem with that. I respect it, and would encourage people who disagree with me to enter into debate so we could hash out our differences, find out precisely where we disagree. I believe I come to the table equipped with documented facts. One of my biggest points of personal pride in this entire saga since I've resigned is that, no matter how much people say they disagree with me, all the reporters who have covered me come back saying the same thing: they cannot prove me wrong on a point of fact. When I say something occurred, it occurred exactly the way I said.

I feel that what I bring to the table is absolutely essential to this debate. That's why I speak out – to bring insights to bear that might not otherwise be heard. Rather than being a traitor, I think my speaking out is the most patriotic thing I can do right now. The biggest service I can perform for my country is to facilitate a wider debate and dialogue on the direction regarding Iraq. If it's to be war, then so be it, but at least it will be a war that's been debated openly and fairly, and for which a case has been made using substantive facts. But if those who push for war cannot make their case, the American public needs to be aware of that as well. That's the role I'm playing.

This goes to the heart of what it means to be an American, and what are our responsibilities. Our primary responsibility is not to sit and nod dumbly while elected representatives say whatever they want in Washington D.C. Our duties and responsibilities are to make American democracy function, and American democracy can only function when citizens are involved, when citizens are empowered with facts. My speaking out has everything to do with empowering democracy, and has absolutely nothing to do with treason or betraying my country.

PITT: You've had difficulties with the FBI.

RITTER: I've been very frank with the FBI from day one. The first FBI investigation began back in 1991 after I married my wife. She's a former citizen of the Soviet Union, currently an American citizen. They dropped their investigation in 1992 when they found it was of no concern to the national security of the United States, and never came close to representing a violation of any law. A man meets a woman, and they fall in love. That's it.

Getting the U.N. job was great. The problem was that the CIA became very concerned because here I was, an intelligence officer, no longer under their control and in a position of influence. The FBI was brought in as a vehicle of intimidation. It didn't work. I don't get intimidated. That went onto the back burner, not to emerge until 1996, when, because of the successful relationship I brokered between the United Nations and Israel, we at UNSCOM were starting to be able to gain a certain degree of independence from the CIA. We didn't need their intelligence as much as we had in the past. This was of concern to people who followed the adage, "Information is Power." As long as the CIA was the sole provider of information, the CIA had power and influence over the inspections. They could dictate where, when, and how we went, just by controlling intelligence.

Because we were able to go to Israel for an extremely effective alternate source of information, the CIA lost its influence. They dealt with that by fabricating charges I was somehow spying for the state of Israel. They turned the FBI loose on me, in what continues to be an ongoing investigation.

When I resigned and started speaking out against American policy in Iraq, a third investigation was initiated. I was made aware of it when I decided to make a documentary film in Iraq called *On Shifting Sands*. Now I was no longer being investigated just as an agent of Israel, but of Iraq as well!

PITT: Some people have called you an Iraqi agent, saying you took $400,000 from Iraq to make this film.

RITTER: To make the movie, I formed a film production company and sought investors. Because of the controversial nature of the film, i.e. actually telling the truth in a manner that would irritate the Clinton administration, not many people wanted to back it. No traditional outlet for documentary films – PBS, Frontline, CNN, etc. – wanted to come forward and put money up to back the idea. An American citizen – and I'll emphasize that point – an American citizen of Iraqi origin named Shakir Alkafajii, who runs businesses in Detroit, was willing to put up $400,000 of his own money. Four hundred thousand is not a lot of money for a high quality hour-and-a-half documentary. And the money didn't come to me anyway. It went to the production company. The film actually wound up costing around $486,000. $56,000 came out of my pocket, $30,000 is still owed to another investor. I haven't made any money off the film. It's a great film, I think. Those who see it say it's the best documentary film on Iraq they've seen.

I worked with the FBI on this. I said I'd be happy to talk about their concerns, which boiled down to worries that there might be a quid pro quo arrangement between the Iraqi government and Shakir Alka-fajii: by supporting my film, he'd get some sort of favorable relationship. I told them that if they found this was the case, or if they ever found that the Iraqi government funneled money through him into the film, I'd terminate the film immediately. Not only did they fail to find any dirt on the money, but after the film was over and I showed it to them, they said it was pretty darned good.

The whole accusation I was an Iraqi agent is nonsense. I wore the uniform of a Marine for twelve years. I went to war for my country. I serve my community today. I'm doing all of this not out of sympathy for the people of Iraq but because I love my own country.

APPENDIX I

The quote from Richard Perle regarding the political cost to George W. Bush if he does not go to war with Iraq was taken from a Reuters story dated August 20, 2002 by Jonathan Wright entitled, "Analysis: U.S. Rhetoric on Iraq Puts Credibility On Line."

The information provided in the chapter, "Iraq in the 20th Century: A Brief History," was derived from a number of sources, most prominently from Ramsey Clark's book, *The Fire This Time*.

A variety of National Security Documents have been declassified which describe American intentions and involvement in the Middle East, spanning from 1947 to 1991. These documents can be found on the George Washington University website, here:

http://www.gwu.edu/~nsarchiv/NSAEBB/NSAEBB21/

The *New York Times* article detailing knowledge within the Reagan administration of Saddam Hussein's use of chemical weapons on the battlefield was written by Patrick E. Tyler, published on August 18th, 2002, and was entitled, "Reagan Aided Iraq Despite Use of Gas."

Security Council Resolution 660 (the condemnation of Iraq), Resolution 661 (the implementation of sanctions), and Resolution 687 (the establishment of the UNSCOM weapons inspection teams), along with the Memorandum of Understanding memorializing the Modalities for Sensitive Site Inspections can be found in full on the United Nations website, here:

http://www.un.org

ACKNOWLEDGEMENTS

This book would not have been possible without the helpful and thoughtful participation of Scott Ritter. He took many hours out of his extraordinarily busy schedule to speak with me, and he cannot be thanked enough.

Sunny Miller, of the Traprock Peace Center, facilitated my contact with Scott Ritter, and she has my eternal gratitude.

This book would also not exist without Beau Friedlander of Context Books, who first approached me with the idea. His enthusiasm and dedication have made this project possible.

Beau Friedlander would not be possible without the helpful and thoughtful maintenance provided by his assistant Trevor Bundy.

A number of people assisted me with essential research, and I would like to thank them: Gloria Lalumia of BuzzFlash.com, Ben Ogden, G. Alain Chamot, Alex Baldwin, David Combs, Bill Warner, James Gauuan all helped with this work. A number of people from the forums at The American Prospect and DemocraticUnderground.com provided a great deal of help in this effort, and they deserve my humble appreciation.

If you have received this book from the hand of a

concerned American, thank them for me. If you pass this book on to someone, you have my thanks.